BRAZIL
AN AWAKENING GIANT

DISCOVERING our HERITAGE

by Mark L. Carpenter

DILLON PRESS, INC.
Minneapolis, Minnesota 55415

Acknowledgments

For help and support in preparing this manuscript, the author wishes to thank his wife, Laurie Anne, and his editor, Thomas R. Schneider, at Dillon Press. For assistance in gathering information for this book, thanks are due to the Brazilian Consulate and Trade Bureau of Chicago, the U. S. Consulate in São Paulo, Diane Bechtel of the Missionary Information Bureau, Carla Zanela Fachini of *Ícaro* magazine/ Varig Airlines, the Centro Cultural Brasil—Estados Unidos (São Paulo), and Eliane Bianchini.

For supplying photographs, the author wishes to thank CEBITUR/ICONOS (Rio de Janeiro), American Airlines, Banco do Brasil—Carteira de Comércio Exterior (São Paulo), *Ícaro* magazine/ Varig Airlines, and *O Estado de São Paulo* newspaper.

Additional photographs are reproduced through the courtesy of Victor Banks (© 1987, pages 8, 11, 14, 15, 41, 50, 69, 75) and EMBRATUR, the Brazilian Tourism Board.

Library of Congress Cataloging in Publication Data

Carpenter, Mark..
   Brazil : an awakening giant.

   (Discovering our heritage)
   Bibliography: p.
   Includes index.
   Summary: Discusses the people, traditions, folkways, holidays, family life, foods, schools, sports, recreations, and history of Brazil.
   1. Brazil—Juvenile literature. [1. Brazil]
I. Title. II. Series.
F2508.5.C33   1987   981   87-13417
ISBN 0-87518-366-2

Dillon Press, Inc., 242 Portland Avenue South
Minneapolis, Minnesota 55415

Printed in the United States of America
    3 4 5 6 7 8 9 10 96 95 94 93 92 91 90

Contents

Fast Facts About Brazil

Official Name: *República Federativa do Brasil* (Federative Republic of Brazil).

Capital: Brasília.

Location: South America; Brazil is nearly the same size as the rest of the continent combined. It shares common borders with all other South American countries except Chile and Ecuador.

Area: 3,286,470 square miles (8,511,957 square kilometers); the distances separating the north from the south and the east from the west are almost exactly the same—2,625 miles (4,225 kilometers). Brazil has 6,019 miles (9,687 kilometers) of Atlantic Ocean coastline.

Elevation: *Highest*—a point on Pico da Neblina 9,888 feet (3,014 meters) above sea level. *Lowest*—sea level along the coast.

Population: *Estimated 1987 population*—141,459,000; *Distribution*—73 percent of the people live in or near cities; 27 percent live in rural areas; *Density*—43 persons per square mile (17 per square kilometer).

Form of Government: Federal republic; *Head of Government*—president.

Important Products: —Steel, automobiles, chemicals, ships, shoes, paper, machinery, military equipment and weapons; coffee, cotton, cattle, soybeans, sugarcane, oranges, bananas; chromium, iron ore, manganese, tin.

Basic Unit of Money: Cruzado.

Official Language: Portuguese.

Major Religions: 80 percent of Brazilians are Roman Catholic. Many, however, are Catholic in name only, and practice "folk Catholicism" or other forms of spiritism. Protestants make up a small— 12 percent—but growing part of the population.

Flag: A yellow diamond on a field of green. Centered inside the diamond is a blue globe containing the words *Ordem e Progresso* ("Order and Progress") and twenty-three white stars—one for each state.

National Anthem: *"O Hino Nacional"* ("The National Hymn").

Major Holidays: New Year's Day—January 1; Carnaval—the Monday and Tuesday preceding Ash Wednesday; Good Friday; Easter Sunday; Tiradentes's Day—April 21; Labor Day—May 1; Independence Day—September 7; The Day of the Dead—November 2; Proclamation of the Republic Day—November 15; Christmas Day—December 25.

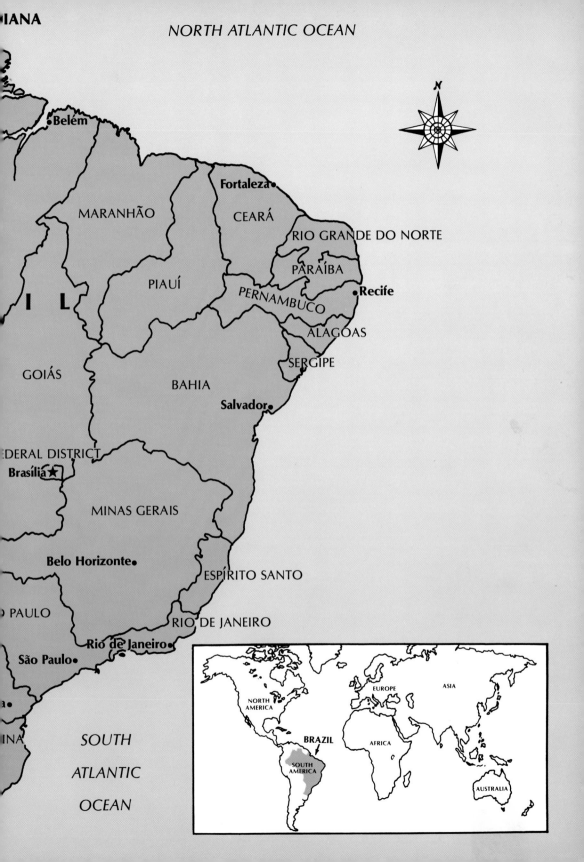

1. Brazil: Jewel of the South

Nearly five hundred years ago, Pedro Álvares Cabral, a sea captain from Portugal, set sail with his crew for India. After a few weeks at sea, they sighted a large mass of land. At first Cabral thought they had reached India. After examining his maps and charts, though, he realized the ship had been sailing in the wrong direction. When the captain and crew went ashore, they discovered a land of rich soil and lush vegetation—in particular, many *pau brasil* (brazilwood) trees. The new land became known as the "Land of the Brazilwood." Later, the Portuguese shortened the name to Brazil.

Cabral didn't realize it, but he had discovered what was to become a very large country. Brazil today is the world's fifth-largest nation. Located in South America, it is almost as big as the rest of the continent put together. Brazil is slightly smaller than the United States.

Because most of Brazil lies below the equator, its seasons are the opposite of those of North America. For example, Brazilians have their winter from June until September each year. Unlike the United States, the northern areas of Brazil are the warmest, while the south has the coolest weather.

Brazil is a land of immense variety and surprising

The Brazilian coast.

contrasts. Tropical jungles and modern cities; large swamplands and dry wastelands; Stone Age Indians and computer operators; dugout canoes and supersonic jets—all are part of Brazil today.

The Mighty Amazon

The Federative Republic of Brazil has twenty-three states, three territories, and one federal district. In Amazonas, the nation's enormous northern state, the great Amazon River winds through vast, thick jungles and rain forests of towering trees and abundant wildlife. The Amazon region holds about one-fifth of the world's fresh water, and its plants produce about one-third of the earth's oxygen. Only the Nile River in Africa is longer than the 3,900 miles (6,275 kilometers) of the Amazon. Parts of this incredible river are so deep that scientists have never been able to measure them.

Thousands of types of fish and plants live in the Amazon. The best-known Amazon fish is the small but deadly *piranha*, which uses its long, sharp teeth to devour other larger fish. Sometimes piranhas attack land animals that venture into the river to cool off or drink. These fish have even been known to bite off the fingers and toes of humans. Other river dwellers are the electric eel—which can deliver a shock of more than 500 volts!—crocodiles, and the monstrous *pirarucú* fish.

Ships such as this one travel along the Amazon River in northern Brazil. The great river has long served as a link between coastal Brazil and the interior.

The Amazon region is the home of many unusual and colorful animals. The capybara (above), *the world's largest rodent, weighs as much as 100 pounds (45.5 kilograms). The parrotlike* arara (right) *flies among the tall trees of the Amazon jungle.*

The steaming tropical jungles that surround the Amazon River are alive with animals. Beneath the jungle canopy live colorful birds such as parrots and toucans, as well as giant rodents, foot-wide butterflies, and *onças,* or spotted leopards.

Two animals rarely seen in the Amazon Basin are the onça, *or spotted leopard* (left), *and the river otter* (above). *The beautifully colored leopard perches on a tree branch, while the otter feeds in the river shallows.*

Although the Amazon region covers more than half of the country, only 7 percent of the people live there. Many small tribes of Indians dwell in the Amazon area. Today, as in centuries past, they live in huts and hunt with spears and bows and arrows. The *serin-*

gueiros of Amazonas, who collect sap from rubber trees, have a very unusual job. These adventurous workers gather the sap from wild rubber trees in the rain forest and sell it to rubber refiners to be made into tires, balls, and other products. In recent years other adventurers, the *garimpeiros*, have come to the Amazon area in search of gold. Brazilians by the thousands dig up and carry the earth from huge mines that hold some of the world's richest gold deposits. All this new development threatens the way of life of the native Indian peoples.

Fishing Villages and Wild West Towns

The northeastern area of Brazil, known as the *nordeste*, is much different than Amazonas. Here there are few jungles, and the weather is much harsher. In some parts of the nordeste, the sun beats down month after month, drying up plants and making it impossible to grow crops. Dry spells can last for as long as three or four years. When the rain finally does come, the heavy downpours last for weeks and often cause serious flooding.

Most of the *nordestinos*—people who live in the northeast—have houses near the Atlantic Ocean where the weather is not as hot. Many nordestinos work as fishermen. They use homemade sailing rafts to cast their huge nets into the sea.

*Fishing boats surround this seaside market port in the north-
eastern city of Belém. Fish and shellfish provide jobs and food
for the people of this region of Brazil.*

Central Brazil is made up of three states—Mato
Grosso, Mato Grosso do Sul, and Minas Gerais. Parts
of the Mato Grosso states are covered by swamps, while
other parts look much like the American towns of the
Wild West days. Many villagers in Mato Grosso walk
around with guns and knives hanging from their hips.

Minas Gerais was one of the first Brazilian states to
be developed. Here are several old colonial cities, such
as Congonhas do Campo and Ouro Preto, filled with

ancient buildings and historic statues. Minas Gerais lies at the heart of Brazil's mining region, where iron ore, chromium, manganese, and many precious metals and stones are taken from the earth. In the state's capital, Belo Horizonte, gem dealers sell sparkling amethysts, emeralds, topazes, and aquamarines. The citizens of Minas Gerais may work in an iron or gold mine or in a rock quarry.

Riches of the South

The south, Brazil's most developed and industrialized area, is home to more than half of the country's 140 million people. In the south, the weather is moderate and comfortable. Farmers till the rich land, planting coffee, beans, sugarcane, soybeans, and other crops. Most of Brazil's large cities are in this region. The people work on farms and ranches, and in the offices and factories of the crowded urban areas.

In the southern states, winter temperatures can dip below the freezing point once in a while. During the winter of 1976, the people of the southern city of Curitiba woke up to a big surprise. Their city was covered by a blanket of white snow! Most of the people had seen snow only on picture postcards of Europe and North America. But it didn't take long for the children to figure out what to do with it. Before long they were

Workers inspect a row of coffee trees in southern Brazil. Brazil is the world's largest producer of coffee.

having snowball fights and making little Brazilian snowmen!

The southern state of Rio Grande do Sul shares a border with Argentina and Uruguay. Here thousands of Brazilian cowboys, called *gaúchos*, herd cattle on the open plains. The gaúchos wear broad-brimmed hats and leather trousers. At night they gather around campfires to eat *churrasco* (barbecued beef), and drink *chimarron*, a strong tea made in hollowed-out gourds and sipped through silver straws.

Brazil produces more coffee than any other nation, and most of it is grown in the south. At harvest time, white-shirted coffee pickers fill the fields. Pickers place large sheets on the ground beneath the ten-feet-high (three-meter-high) coffee trees. Then they strip off the coffee beans with glove-clad hands, gather the beans from the sheets, and place them in bags. Most of this important crop is sent to nations around the world.

Many large factories have been built in southern Brazil. Some of these manufacturing plants produce cars, trucks, and farm equipment that are exported to countries worldwide. Other exports include shoes, textiles, construction equipment, and leather products. Many of these products are shipped to the United States, Brazil's largest trading partner.

São Paulo rises at the heart of Brazil's industrial region. The largest city in South America, São Paulo has 8 million residents—15 million in the metropolitan area. A modern city, it has many freeways, subways, shopping centers, and high-rise office buildings.

São Paulo is the home of *Instituto Butantan*, a large snake farm. At this world famous institute, poisonous snakes of all colors and sizes are "milked" for their venom. Trained milkers carefully pick up the snakes and extract the poison from the sharp fangs. The venom is then used to make life-saving snakebite serums that are sent to countries worldwide. The institute also dis-

At night towering skyscrapers in the huge city of São Paulo form glittering rows of bright lights.

plays hundreds of other reptiles, as well as scorpions, spiders, and other poisonous insects.

São Paulo's subway system is one of the world's most modern. Spotlessly clean, its trains, ticket machines, and escalators are usually in perfect working order. Passengers rarely have to wait more than five minutes for a train. Even though robbery and other crimes are common in São Paulo, the subways remain remarkably free from the "work" of pickpockets and purse snatchers.

Rio de Janeiro—often called simply "Rio"—is Brazil's second-largest city. Called the *Cidade Maravilhosa* ("Marvelous City"), Rio attracts people from all over Brazil and the world. Located on beautiful Guanabara Bay, an inlet of the Atlantic Ocean, it is surrounded by large, sprawling beaches. Here people enjoy sunbathing, swimming, surfing, playing soccer, and flying huge birdlike kites. The *cariocas*—the citizens of Rio—are in love with their city. Many people consider Rio de Janeiro to be the most beautiful of all the world's cities.

Unfortunately, it is known not only for its beauty, but also for its thieves. Residents and visitors alike have discovered that it is unsafe to go out into the streets or beaches of Rio carrying money, a camera, jewelry, a watch, or anything else of value. The young thieves often steal these items in broad daylight. There are so many of these *trombadinhas*—"little crashes," a term

The high-rise buildings and white-sand beaches of Rio de Janeiro lie along Guanabara Bay, an inlet of the Atlantic Ocean.

used to refer to the young robbers—that the police find it nearly impossible to catch them all.

The world's largest soccer stadium, the Maracanã, located in downtown Rio de Janeiro, seats 200,000 fans. Brazil's national pastime is soccer. Known worldwide

for excellent *futebol*—the Portuguese word for soccer—
Brazil has won countless international championships.

Curitiba, in the southern state of Paraná, looks like
a classic European city and has a mild, usually cool
climate. Its residents appreciate music and art and hold
several music festivals each year. Often famous artists
come here to paint blank billboards while crowds watch
below.

Every Saturday morning in Curitiba, city workers
take a huge roll of paper to a downtown sidewalk. They
unroll it down an entire block. Young people of all ages
appear, and each is given a paintbrush and jars of paint.
The boys and girls may paint anything they want on
their section of the roll of paper. Later the long strips
of colorfully painted paper are displayed in public
buildings.

A Young and Modern Capital

During the 1960s, Brazil's new national capital,
Brasília, was built about 600 miles (970 kilometers)
from the Atlantic coast to encourage people to settle the
country's vast inland areas. The city, which is a federal
district like Washington, D.C., was planned so that it
developed in the shape of an enormous airplane. The
residential section forms one wing, the commercial section lies in another, and all the federal government

Brazil's modern capital, Brasília, was planned so that it developed in the shape of an enormous airplane. Federal government buildings can be seen in this view of the city.

buildings are grouped in yet another section. Brasília is one of the most carefully planned cities in the world. Noted architects such as Brazil's Oscar Niemeyer designed many of its modern buildings. Even though the capital is very young, more than half a million people now live there.

Brazil's president and Congress, made up of the Senate and the Chamber of Deputies, meet in Brasília's federal government buildings. In the past, military leaders have played an important part in Brazil's government. Although military officers ruled the nation from 1964 to 1985, the country now has a civilian president and elects its government leaders. A 1985 constitutional amendment provides for the direct election of future presidents by the Brazilian people.

Brazilians have worked hard to make their country what it is today. The rapid growth of manufacturing and agriculture have made the nation a world economic power. Despite the tremendous growth, most Brazilians are still poor, whether they live in a remote rural area or in a city slum. If the country continues to achieve strong economic growth, many of these people may join the small but rapidly growing middle class and share the wealth of their nation. Today, though, the rich and the poor of Brazil live in two separate and very different worlds.

2. Rags and Riches

A "melting pot" is a place where people of all races and nationalities live together. This term describes Brazil. During the last two hundred years, people have come from all over the world to live in the largest South American nation. As a result, today many Brazilians look like Europeans, Asians, Africans, and Middle Easterners. Brazil is a country where anyone can feel at home. Brazilians may be white, black, Hispanic, Asian, or of mixed ancestry. The only "purely" Brazilian people are the native Indians, who today number 150,000.

Most immigrants to Brazil have not tried to live in their own communities, separated from other Brazilians. In the cities, there are no neighborhoods called "Little Italy" or "Chinatown" or "Greek Village," such as those in other large cities of the world. People who move to Brazil usually live among their neighbors, regardless of their national origins.

Brazilians of different races often marry each other. Because of this mixing, social scientists say that a new race is being created in Brazil. It is a race made up of all other races.

Although Brazilians have varied ethnic backgrounds, they do share some common beliefs, customs,

Brazilian people today reflect a variety of ethnic backgrounds. The boy (left) *balancing the basket on his head is the descendant of African slaves. The sculptor-painter* (above) *is a European immigrant.*

and characteristics. Most believe in God. At least eight out of ten Brazilians belong to the Roman Catholic church, though many of them do not actively practice their religion. Spiritism, another of Brazil's main religions, combines the Catholic faith with African spiritual beliefs. Spiritists hold elaborate rituals in which spirits of the dead are said to enter into the bodies of living people. Spiritist religions such as *candomblé* and *macumba* were brought to Brazil by African slaves many years ago. Portuguese landowners wanted the slaves to work on their plantations.

A Peaceful People

Unlike most other Latin American nations, Brazil has had a peaceful history. This vast country has never fought a full-scale war against another nation, nor has it ever experienced a large-scale civil war. Even its independence from Portugal was won peacefully.

Brazilians do have an interest in politics, but very few are willing to fight for the political party or system they favor. In this respect, Brazilians are different from the people of most other Latin American countries, where violent revolutions have often toppled governments.

In 1984, more than a million people gathered in downtown Rio de Janeiro. Their purpose was to protest certain government actions. But instead of marching down the streets waving signs and screaming angry chants, they listened to a few speeches, and to the music of a symphony orchestra. Then they watched a laser light show and sang popular tunes together. A gathering that could have turned into an angry mob was transformed into an enormous party. For most Brazilians, poor and rich alike, people are more important than politics.

Two Separate Worlds

Poor families throughout Brazil live in unclean, rundown homes, often in crowded city neighborhoods. The slums of Rio de Janeiro and São Paulo are among the world's worst. Called *favelas* by Brazilians, these slums are home to 35 million extremely poor people who live in tiny shacks made of old scraps of wood and metal. Most of these flimsy shacks have dirt floors and no running water. Sometimes an entire family must sleep together on a damp, insect-infested straw mattress. Here the people cook food on crude wood-burning stoves, and wash clothes by hand in polluted creeks or with water taken from community faucets. Because of the unclean conditions, favelas are breeding grounds for plagues and disease. Some poor neighborhoods have become hiding places for thieves and murderers. One such slum in São Paulo is called *Buraco Quente* ("Hot Hole"). Most of the favela dwellers, though, are honest people who cannot afford to live anywhere better.

Even though more than half of Brazil's population lives in extreme poverty, millions of city dwellers belong to the growing middle class. These people can usually afford to buy or rent a modest house or apartment. The houses and apartments are equipped with electricity, running water, indoor bathrooms, and sewer systems.

Like these two boys, many of Brazil's poor people live in crowded city slums known as favelas.

Middle class children attend public schools, unlike favela children, who must often work or beg instead of going to school. Although some middle class people can afford to buy and maintain an economy car, most, like the poor, rely on public transportation. For a small fee—equal to a few U.S. cents—Brazilians can ride on city buses, trains, and subways.

People in Brazil's upper class live in expensive houses or apartments surrounded by armed guards who

*In Rio de Janeiro, signs of wealth such as five-star hotels exist
alongside the extreme poverty of the slums that cling to the steep
sides of nearby hills.*

keep out thieves and trespassers. They drive luxury cars,
and can afford to purchase Brazilian-made freezers,
microwave ovens, videocassette recorders, dishwashers,
and personal computers. These people live in a world
that is set apart from the world of the favela dwellers.
The two worlds rarely meet.

Nowhere in the world is there a greater difference
between the rich and the poor than in Brazil. In Rio de
Janeiro a miserable favela clings to a hillside, directly

across the street from a dazzling five-star hotel. Everywhere the symbols of wealth—glimmering mansions, Mercedes automobiles, and designer clothing—exist alongside the telltale signs of poverty—shantytowns, half-dressed dirty beggars, and paper collectors pushing their wooden carts through the downtown streets.

In the large cities of Brazil, hundreds of thousands of abandoned children roam the streets. These young people may be orphans with no place to go, or they may have been pushed out of their favela homes by parents or relatives who have no means to feed and care for them. Many of them learn to steal in order to get money for food.

Movies, Music, and Art

In 1982 a major movie appeared about the problem of Brazil's abandoned children. This award-winning film, *Pixote*, told the story of a young boy who escapes from a juvenile detention center and learns to rob and murder in order to survive. The movie showed audiences around the world what it is like to live as an abandoned child in São Paulo. Brazil's government is trying to provide help and homes for these children, but it does not have enough resources to help everyone.

Pixote is just one of the many Brazilian movies that have been made during recent years. Another popular film was *Bye Bye Brazil*, which shows the ways in which foreign television programming and products are changing Brazilian life. In one scene, Amazon Indians are shown wearing Adidas shorts and drinking Coca-Cola!

Brazil has thousands of movie theaters. Children especially like films featuring *Os Trapalhões* ("The Troublemakers"), a group of four crazy misfits who get into all sorts of adventures and mischief. Whenever a new Trapalhões movie is released, children line up by the hundreds to see Renato Aragão and his troublemaking friends.

Popular American movies such as *Star Wars*, *E.T.*, *Top Gun*, and *Rambo* are also big hits in Brazil. When an American movie is shown, subtitles appear at the bottom of the screen, so that people can read in Portuguese what the actors are saying in English.

Brazilians enjoy music as well as movies. Each year countless concerts are staged in small clubs, gymnasiums, and music halls all over the country. The people enjoy many types of music, from the great classical pieces to popular music such as *samba*, *baião*, *pagode*, and *sertaneja*. Like young people all over the world, though, young Brazilians have learned to love rock music. In the 1960s and 1970s, they listened to American and British rock bands. Now many Brazilian music groups play nothing but rock. Among the most popular rock bands in Brazil are RPM, *Ultraje a Rigor* ("For-

The Museu de Arte de São Paulo displays paintings by Rafael and Picasso as well as Brazilian masters.

mal Outrage"), and *Paralamas do Sucesso* ("Fenders of Success").

Other forms of art and entertainment, such as theater, dance, painting, sculpture, and literature, are growing more popular in Brazil. South America's finest art museum, the Museu de Arte de São Paulo, features famous paintings by Rafael and Picasso. It also displays art by Brazilian masters such as Di Cavalcanti, Candido Portinari, and Alfredo Volpi.

A Beautiful Language

Because the Portuguese were the first Europeans to arrive and settle in Brazil, the country's official language today is Portuguese. It is a beautiful language which, when spoken, sounds more like French than Spanish. Like French and Spanish, Portuguese is a Romance language that has its origins in ancient Latin. Here are a few words in Portuguese and Spanish to compare:

SPANISH	PORTUGUESE	ENGLISH
pan	pão	bread
pero	cachorro (or cão)	dog
ventana	janela	window
puerta	porta	door
muchacho	menino (or rapaz)	boy
iglesia	igreja	church
casa	casa	house
ciudad	cidade	city

Even though the Portuguese and Spanish languages are similar, Brazilians are much more interested in learning English than Spanish. By learning English, people have a better chance of succeeding in the business world. Brazil has a close trade relationship with the United States, Canada, Great Britain, and other nations where English is spoken.

One of the first things people notice when they see the favelas in the big cities of Brazil are the glittering pieces of aluminum atop the crowded rooftops—TV antennas! Although favela families sometimes don't have enough to eat, they can watch prime-time *novelas* (soap operas) or soccer matches on television. If they can laugh and dream about how their lives might change, they can keep their hope for the future. Whether they are poor or rich, Brazilians tend to think things will get better. They know how to make the best of their situation, regardless of how bad things might be today. It is this hope, this desire to succeed, that is making Brazil a strong and growing global economic power.

3. A History of Peace

Long before the Europeans came, the Tupí-Guaraní and other Indian groups lived in what is now Brazil. These early people hunted and fished, grew crops, and gathered fruits from the dense forests that covered much of the land. Many Indians had no permanent homes, but some groups lived in villages in large, long thatched houses.

When Captain Pedro Álvares Cabral and his crew arrived in 1500, it didn't take long for the news to get back to Portugal. The Portuguese heard fabulous stories about a faraway tropical paradise full of rich land and precious metals. By the 1530s, colonists began to invade Brazil by the shiploads. It soon became a valuable Portuguese colony.

Portuguese Rule

Many of the people who first came to Brazil were farmers in search of fertile soil and a mild climate. They cleared the coastal land and established large farms, or plantations, to grow sugarcane and spices. The new settlers soon found that they did not have enough workers for their farms. To solve that problem, the Portuguese farmers, who were used to having slaves back home, tried to enslave the local Indians. Some Indians fought the Portuguese and were killed. Those who were captured had never worked so hard under the hot tropical sun, and many of them became ill and died.

Because they were unsuccessful with the Indians, the plantation owners decided to use Africans as slaves. Portuguese slave traders brought many thousands of black Africans to Brazil and sold them to farmers. With these slaves working hard day after day, the plantations soon produced abundant crops. Sold in Europe, Brazilian sugarcane, cotton, and tobacco helped produce great wealth for Portugal.

In the 1690s and early 1700s, adventurers discovered huge deposits of gold and diamonds in Brazil's interior. These newfound riches caused a mad rush to the area known today as the states of Minas Gerais, which means "General Mines," and Mato Grosso. The miners brought in African slaves, who dug up many tons of gold, diamonds, amethysts, topazes, aquamarines, and other precious and semi-precious stones.

When the king of Portugal realized what a treasure the miners had discovered, he began to send colorfully dressed *bandeirantes* ("flag bearers") out in every direction to mark the boundaries of the new country. These determined explorers went so far in staking claims and planting flags for Portugal that they covered half of the

Today, as in centuries past, adventurers travel to Brazil's interior regions in search of gold, diamonds, and other valuable metals and precious stones. These boys have staked a claim of their own.

South American continent. Spain, the other major South American colonial power, did not know how far the flag bearers had traveled. Because of their efforts, Portugal and Spain signed the Treaty of Madrid in 1750. That treaty established Brazil's boundaries close to where they are today, and divided South America between the two European colonial powers.

Portugal ruled Brazil for almost three hundred years. After a while it became clear that Portugal did not want Brazil to become an independent country. The Portuguese wanted only to take Brazil's rich mineral and agricultural wealth back to their native land. As a result, they did not build schools and universities in Brazil, and did not permit factories or industries to be established there.

The Struggle for Independence

Under Portuguese rule, most Brazilians were poor, overworked, and underfed. They earned very little for long hours of hard work. In the late 1700s some Brazilian men began to hold secret meetings in small towns in the state of Minas Gerais. They were unhappy with what the Portuguese were doing to Brazil, and started to make plans to overthrow the imperial government.

One of the leaders was a dentist named Joaquim José da Silva Xavier. Everyone called him by his nick-

Rebels plotting Brazil's independence from Portugal held secret meetings in the town of Ouro Preto in the state of Minas Gerais. Today the city is considered a historic landmark.

name, *Tiradentes*, which means "Tooth Puller." Tiradentes wanted Brazil to be a free country, and he tried to persuade other Brazilians to join him in this fight. One of the men he talked to did not agree with his ideas and turned Tiradentes over to Portuguese officials. Tiradentes was arrested, along with several of his friends.

When they stood before the judge, all of Tiradentes's friends denied that they had anything to do with the illegal independence movement. Only Tiradentes stood up for what he believed in and told the truth. On April 31, 1792, he was condemned to death by hanging.

Today the people of Brazil consider Tiradentes one of their great heroes. Every April 21, they celebrate Tiradentes Day and remember his fight for freedom.

Early in the nineteenth century, events in Europe began to affect the Brazilian struggle for independence. In 1807, France, led by Napoleon Bonaparte, invaded Portugal because it had supported Britain in a war between the French and the British. Portugal's royal family fled to Brazil, where the king, Dom João VI, was immediately hailed as the new ruler. Brazil, which had been a Portuguese colony until then, was now considered the headquarters of the government of Portugal. Dom João VI ruled from 1808 to 1821.

When the French were defeated and driven from Portugal, Dom João decided to return to his homeland. Yet as he boarded the ship in Rio de Janeiro, many Brazilians were angry at him. They suspected that his ships were full of Brazilian gold. By now most people knew that Portugal was interested in Brazil only because of its valuable crops and minerals. They were glad to see Dom João leave.

The Portuguese king knew the Brazilians were angry, and that they would soon demand complete freedom from Portugal. He left his son, Dom Pedro I, as the official ruler of Brazil.

On April 21, a national holiday known as Tiradentes Day, students from Colegio Tiradentes high school clean the towering statue of Brazil's national hero.

Dom Pedro I felt more loyalty to the country of Brazil than to Portugal. Since he knew the Brazilians wanted freedom, he decided to break all ties with Portugal. On September 7, 1822, on the banks of the Ipiranga River, Dom Pedro raised his sword into the air and shouted, "Independence or death!" Portugal, in no condition to fight because of its loss to France, granted the country its independence.

The Empire

Dom Pedro I was declared king of the empire of Brazil. Yet even though he considered himself a Brazilian, the king did not have much to do with his people. Instead, he chose to live in magnificent palaces that the new government could barely afford to maintain. The king also permitted the rich Brazilian landowners to keep all their slaves. Dom Pedro I ruled the country so badly that in 1831 the Brazilians forced him to give up the throne in favor of his son, who was only five years old!

Nine years later, at the age of fourteen, Dom Pedro II became the second emperor of Brazil. During his reign many factories were built. The country began to produce coffee to supply Europe, where the beverage had been introduced by the Arabs in the seventeenth century.

Although Dom Pedro II ruled Brazil well, the people resented living in poverty while their leaders possessed great wealth. During this period the Brazilian antislavery movement strengthened. The movement's growing strength led to the 1888 signing of the *Lei Áurea*, a law that granted freedom to the slaves. Freedom under the law, though, did not mean that blacks were made equal in Brazilian society. Blacks were rarely given full-time jobs and had to fight for odd jobs in order to survive.

Along with the antislavery movement, a movement toward democracy was born. The old Portuguese-style royal ruler failed to keep pace with the rapid economic and social advances the country had made. On November 15, 1889, Brazil became a republic. Dom Pedro II and the royal family were sent back to Portugal.

Democracy and Dictators

For forty-one years Brazilians lived in a democracy in which a few powerful leaders held most political power. They patterned their constitution and government after the American model. Then in 1930 Getúlio Vargas seized power with the help of the Brazilian army. He wrote a new constitution that increased wages, shortened work hours, and gave labor unions new rights. Later, though, he ruled the nation as a dictator.

In 1945 Vargas was overthrown in another military coup. Five years later he regained power, this time legally. He tried to create more freedoms for the people, supporting the creation of labor unions and allowing freedom of the press. Brazil's military leaders, however, did not support him. On August 24, 1954, Vargas grew tired of fighting. He put a revolver to his heart and killed himself.

Soon afterward, Juscelino Kubitschek was elected president. Kubitschek is known as the man who built Brasília. Until 1960 the capital of Brazil was Rio de Janeiro. Since most of Brazil's cities were located along the Atlantic coastline, Kubitschek decided to pick a spot far inland to become the capital. He believed the capital's presence there would boost the development of Brazil's vast interior. Today Brasília is a thriving young city and has caused many Brazilians to consider moving to the nation's new inland frontier areas.

After Kubitschek, the nation's next president was Jânio Quadros, who resigned after seven months in power. The vice-president, João Goulart, then became president. Shortly after Goulart took office, he was accused of being a Communist. Brazil's military leaders feared that his policies would lead to a Communist takeover. In 1964 the military overthrew Goulart and set up a new form of government—a military dictatorship—which lasted for twenty-one years. During this

period several general-presidents passed laws that pro-
hibited freedom of speech and of the press. People who
criticized the government were jailed, often tortured,
and sometimes killed.

Even though Brazil had serious economic and social problems during the years of military rule, this
period was also a time of great economic growth. New
industries thrived, and agricultural exports brought
more money to Brazil than the country had ever re-
ceived. Leaders began to invest in large development
projects such as nuclear power plants, superhighways,
and hydroelectric dams. Due to open in the early 1990s,
the Itaipú Dam Power Plant will be the world's most
powerful hydroelectric plant. Brazil borrowed billions
of dollars from foreign banks to help pay for these
projects.

When a worldwide oil shortage developed during
the mid-1970s, Brazil's growth was stopped short. As in
the United States and other countries, Brazil's economy
was hurt by high oil prices. The nation had to find new
ways to pay off its huge debts to foreign banks. During
this period, many Brazilians lost faith in the military
rulers. They called for a change in leadership.

In the early 1980s, President João Baptista Figuei-
redo, the last of the military dictators, agreed to turn the
government over to civilian (nonmilitary) leaders. In
early 1985, after a long campaign, Brazil's Congress

When completed, the Itaipú Dam Power Plant (left) *will produce more power than any other hydroelectric plant in the world. Tancredo Neves* (above) *led Brazil back to democracy after twenty-one years of military rule. He suddenly became ill and died before taking office.*

voted to name Tancredo de Almeida Neves to the presidency. The people of Brazil were overjoyed. This man, a deeply religious ex-governor, was a popular leader. Sadly, Tancredo Neves never became president. The night before he was scheduled to take office, he was hospitalized with a serious infection. Six weeks later he died.

The New Republic

All of Brazil mourned. Their new leader, the man who was to lead the country back to democracy, lay dead. The vice-president, José Sarney, solemnly took office, vowing to pursue the same ideals Tancredo Neves held. President Sarney promised to lead what he called the *Nova República* ("New Republic") back to economic recovery and democracy.

Sarney inherited many problems from the previous military government. Some were so deep-rooted that no one was quite sure how to handle them. For example, many elected officials took money for themselves from funds meant to help poor people. Brazil had serious economic problems such as high inflation, or rapidly increasing prices. To make matters worse, Brazil owed $100 billon to foreign banks, and there was no way to pay off this debt.

President Sarney began a number of economic reforms aimed at solving several of these difficult problems. Some of his policies had a positive effect, while others failed. Early in 1987, the government announced that it could no longer make the $12 billion annual interest payments on the national debt. After a brief slowdown, prices began to rise rapidly again.

In 1988, the Brazilian Congress adopted a new constitution for Brazil. A constitution reflects a country's fundamental beliefs, ideals, and laws. It serves as a standard which all citizens are expected to follow. Brazilians hope that the new constitution will help their nation develop in a way that will benefit all its people.

A year after the new national constitution was adopted, Brazilians held their first free elections for president in nearly thirty years. On December 17, 1989, Fernando Collor de Mello won the election. Collor faced severe economic and social problems when he took office early in 1990.

The new president, just forty years old when he took office, launched a program of "shock therapy" for the Brazilian economy. He planned to put an end to the very high rate of inflation by balancing the government's budget. Collor announced programs to cut the size of government agencies and to sell many state-owned companies to private investors. He hoped to encourage private investment in Brazil's economy to help it grow.

Each year Brazil's population grows rapidly. To keep pace with the young people entering the work force, the nation needs to create 2 million new jobs each year. To create that many jobs, the economy has to grow at a rapid rate. At the same time, the government is trying to make payments to reduce the foreign debt. If Collor's government does not succeed, the number of poor and jobless Brazilians will continue to grow. If his

São Paulo lies at the center of Brazil's modern industrial region. Here, as elsewhere, more than half of the cars run on alcohol fuel produced from the juice of Brazilian sugarcane.

programs work, then the country may be able to solve some of its problems. More poor Brazilians may be able to join the nation's growing middle class of workers.

Brazil has been called a highly self-sufficient nation. This means that much of what its people consume—from food and clothing to automobile fuel and manufactured goods—is grown or mined or made within the country. Many Brazilians believe that depending on their own products and resources will help their nation pay its debt and continue to make economic progress.

In recent years Brazil has become more self-sufficient by developing an unusual source of home-grown energy. Rather than depending on imported oil to produce gasoline, Brazilians developed the technology for alcohol-run cars. Today more than half of Brazil's automobiles run on 100 percent alcohol. This fuel is made from the juice of sugarcane, an abundant crop well suited to large areas of the country.

Because Brazil was founded by people who were interested mainly in robbing its resources, its people have suffered for many years. Today, despite its problems, Brazil is a country that looks toward the future. Brazilians have elected their own president and representatives. Their government is working hard to solve economic problems and create jobs for the nation's poor. Factories are producing and exporting everything from shoes to microcomputers. Brazil now has the resources, both natural and human, to become one of the world's great nations.

4. Myths and Sayings

The people of Brazil have created a rich collection of myths and legends that reflect their country's natural wonders and religious heritage. Many of the stories had their origins among the Indian peoples of the Amazon region. These native Brazilians believe that hundreds of spirits—good and evil—dwell in the jungle and influence their lives.

Amazon Legends

One of the Indians' legends explains the existence of the *vitória régia*, the enormous lily pads that float in and around the Amazon River. Some of these lily pads are so large that they will withstand the weight of a small child without sinking. The Indians believe that the vitória régia are the transformed bodies of Indian women who have drowned in the river.

One of the most popular soft drinks in Brazil is called *guaraná*. It is a delicious drink made from the juice of the guaraná berry. The Amazon Indians tell a story that describes how the guaraná fruit came to be.

They say that many years ago an Indian couple asked Tupã, the king of the gods, to give them a child.

Indians in the Amazon region believe that these vitória régia—
*giant floating lily pads—are actually the transformed bodies of
drowned Indian women.*

Their wish was granted, and soon the woman gave birth
to a beautiful baby boy. The boy was intelligent, strong,
and kind. Everyone in the tribe grew to love him.

The child was so well liked that he made Jurupari,
an evil spirit, jealous and angry. Jurupari decided to do
away with the boy. He turned into a snake and waited
for the right moment. One day the boy wandered into
the woods to gather fruit. When he neared the bushes,
the snake bit him, and the boy fell to the ground dead.

When the Indians noticed that the boy was gone, they went out looking for him. The searchers found his body near the bushes. As they gathered around him to grieve, a flash of lightning struck the ground nearby.

Seeing this, the boy's mother said, "That was a sign from Tupã, the king of the gods. He has had mercy on us. If we plant the eyes of our boy in the soil, a fruit will rise up which will bring us great happiness."

The Indians did as she instructed. Sure enough, after a few weeks, a plant came out of the ground. It bore a red berry with a black dot surrounded by a thin white film. The Indians named the fruit "guaraná," which in their language means "berries that look like human eyes."

A Sleeping Giant

One of Brazil's most interesting legends comes from the inhabitants of Rio de Janeiro. If you sailed into Guanabara Bay, and saw the mountains and ridges that surround the city, you would soon see that all these geographic features look like the enormous outline of a sleeping man. Different features combine to form the "head," the "chest," and the entire "sleeping body."

As the legend goes, this shadowy outline of a man was once a giant who was given the task of protecting Guanabara Bay. One day he murdered a beautiful Indi-

Many residents of Rio de Janeiro believe that the outline of a sleeping giant can be seen in the mountains and ridges surrounding Guanabara Bay.

an girl, and God turned him into stone. Fishermen in Guanabara Bay say that once in a while the giant arises and walks about. On such occasions, he summons the clouds and fogs so that nobody will see he has moved.

Watch Out for the Saci

Perhaps the most well known legendary figure in Brazil is the *Saci-Pererê*. Many rural Brazilians are

absolutely sure that this creature exists. They say the
Saci is a black boy who has only one leg, fire-red eyes,
and a swollen stomach. He has pointed ears, wears
nothing but a long red stocking cap on his head, and
smokes a corncob pipe. He runs—or hops—as fast as
lightning, has the ability to appear and disappear at will,
and can make himself large or small. When he sees
humans, he lets out a high-pitched whistle, sticks out his
tongue, and shoots smoke out his ears.

The Saci lives in the woods behind farms, and no
one knows where he will show up next. His favorite
activity is to disturb and attack horses. When a horse is
alone, the Saci will rope it and jump on its back, grab-
bing the horse's neck tightly. Then he bites into the
horse's neck and feeds on the blood. The next day, the
horse seems very tired, as if it has galloped ten miles
without stopping.

The Saci also likes to make life difficult for humans.
If he encounters a man traveling alone at night, he will
whistle loudly into his ear to frighten him. Then he will
tickle and slap the man senseless. Sometimes the Saci
doesn't slap the traveler, but knocks his hat off, scares
his horse, and makes the saddle slip.

In farmhouses the Saci sometimes pulls off people's
covers, pulls their hair, and throws ashes into children's
eyes. He gets into all sorts of trouble and makes everyone's life miserable.

The most famous character of Brazilian myths and legends, the Saci Pererê, is known for his mischief and troublemaking.

Nevertheless, Brazilians believe it is not hard to get rid of the Saci. To do it, a person needs a Catholic rosary or saint's statue to hold in his presence. Then, if the person recites the Catholic creed while holding the rosary or statue, the Saci will whistle loudly and disappear, never to return again.

When Brazilian children misbehave, their mothers may tell them to straighten up or else the *Bicho Papão* will get them. The Bicho Papão is an imaginary mon-

ster. A popular lullaby that mothers sing to young
children, *Nana Nenê*, goes like this in English:

> Sleep, baby, sleep
> Or the "Bicho" will get you;
> Daddy's out working on the farm
> And your mommy's gone out for a walk.

Sayings and Superstitions

Most Brazilians enjoy clever sayings and proverbs
and use them in their daily lives. Truck drivers often
paint such sayings on the bumpers or mudflaps of their
trucks. One of their favorites is *Pé na tábua e fé em
Deus*. This means "Floor the accelerator and have faith
in God!" In other words, "Go as fast as you can, but
don't forget to ask God for protection."

Many popular sayings involve animals. For example, when someone wants to make the point that each
person has unique tastes and talents, he or she might
say, *Cada macaco no seu galho* ("Every monkey on his
own branch").

When someone gets into trouble for talking too
much, a friend might scold him or her by saying, *Em
boca fechada não entra mosca* ("Flies don't enter a
closed mouth!").

One often-heard saying is *Quem tem boca vai à Roma* ("If you have a mouth, you can go to Rome"). This means you can always get to where you are headed if you are willing to ask for directions along the way.

People all over the world have superstitions, but some of the strangest are held by Brazilians. Many will not take a shower or a bath immediately after a meal, fearing it would do great harm to their digestive systems. Some mothers warn their children not to drink milk after eating a mango, because the combination may kill them. And for some reason nobody quite understands, it is unhealthy to drink coffee while looking into a mirror.

Farm people in Brazil are especially fond of folk cures for physical and emotional illnesses. One such "cure" deals with warts. If you have warts, they say, you should take a large piece of meat and rub it on them. Then take the meat and bury it inside an anthill. When the ants have completely eaten the meat, your warts will disappear!

Many Brazilians no longer believe in all these legends, superstitions, and folk cures. As they move to the city, go to school, and learn about the laws of science, the stories they grew up with no longer have the same meaning. And yet, the folktales and legends remain a valuable part of Brazil's national character and cultural heritage.

5. Samba and Celebrations

Brazil is known for the way it celebrates its holidays. In fact, the Brazilian people are experts at having fun. For them, a holiday is a time to wear their best clothes, to gather together with many friends, and celebrate!

Carnaval Time

The greatest holiday celebration, known as *Carnaval*, takes place about six weeks before Easter during the days leading up to Lent. For religious Christians, Lent is a serious time for thinking about the meaning of Jesus' last days on earth. Just before Lent begins, though, Brazilians celebrate Carnaval with a party on a truly grand scale. Everyone wears colorful costumes, samba music is everywhere, and people dance in the streets.

The Brazilian people view Carnaval as a time to forget the dull, difficult, and unpleasant things of life. It is a time to pretend. The poor man puts on fancy clothes and pretends he is rich. The workers and the slum dwellers play loud musical instruments and pretend they don't have a care in the world. Everyone wears colorful costumes, disguises, and masks. Children pretend they are clowns, princesses, or witches.

For Brazilians, such as this young woman, Carnaval is a time to put on a colorful costume and celebrate.

After dressing up for Carnaval, Brazilians go to clubs and ballrooms where they can dance and play to the rhythms of samba music. In many cities, entire streets are roped off to make plenty of room for the dancers.

Carnaval couldn't exist in Brazil without the powerful rhythms of samba. This form of music is played by dozens of musicians who play all shapes and sizes of drums, rattles, and tambourines. One instrument looks like a small frying pan and is hit repeatedly with a piece of metal. The most unusual instrument is the *cuíca*, which makes a yelping, mournful sound that can sound like a wounded animal or even a human. All the musicians are led by a single director who blows a whistle to signal stops or rhythm changes. The rhythm is so loud and involving that people automatically start swaying and dancing to it.

In Brazil's largest cities, such as Rio, São Paulo, and Salvador, people organize themselves into "samba schools." These large organizations have as many as 3,000 members. Each "school" parades through a specially prepared downtown street, showing off its costumes, dances, and rhythm sections. The schools compete against each other and are judged by a panel of experts. Prizes are awarded for such categories as best samba song, best theme, best dance, and best costume. The largest samba schools spend hundreds of thou-

During Carnaval, the loud rhythms of samba music can be heard throughout Brazil. Here, a Rio "samba school" featuring hundreds of musicians and dancers puts on a dazzling show of color and sound.

sands of dollars each year to buy and decorate instruments, costumes, and floats.

Rio's Carnaval celebration is the most well known one in Brazil, and in the world. Each year thousands of tourists—from within Brazil and from many other countries—come to see the festival. In the past, Rio's samba-school contest was held on a downtown avenue along which huge bleachers were erected. The bleachers were torn down again just a week later. Several years ago, the mayor of Rio de Janeiro ordered the construction of the permanent Sambódromo, a huge, reinforced concrete outdoor viewing stand for the four-day event.

The Carnaval celebrations last all night long and, in some cities, continue during the daytime hours as well. Everything starts closing down late in the night before Ash Wednesday, the first day of Lent. Now it's time for people to remember who they are, put on their regular clothes, and go back to their normal life, as if the wild days of singing and dancing had never happened.

Easter and the June Festivals

Since most Brazilians are Catholic, all traditional Christian holidays are observed. During Holy Week, which ends with Easter Sunday, a number of religious processions and celebrations are held throughout the country. In the old colonial towns near the gold mines of Minas Gerais, such as Diamantina, Congonhas do Campo, and Ouro Preto, these processions are very big events. Long lines of people walk through the towns' steep cobblestone streets, chanting mournful songs in memory of Christ's death.

Brazilians celebrate Easter in much the same way as North Americans. They hold special Sunday sunrise services in Catholic and Protestant churches. Children eat special chocolates and play with Easter eggs.

Children lead an Easter parade through the streets of a town in northeastern Brazil.

In June several religious holy days occur—Saint Anthony's Day, Saint Peter's Day, Saint John's Day, and days dedicated to other saints. During this month Brazilians have many parties and festivals, called the June Festivals. These celebrations are especially popular among children, who dress up in old-fashioned plaid clothes, paint freckles on their faces, and wear oversized straw hats. At the June Festivals people dance the *quadrilha*, a Brazilian square dance, to the sound of *sertaneja*, a type of music popular in Brazil's interior.

Since June is the first month of Brazil's winter, in the south it can be quite cold during this time of year. At the June Festivals, people eat and drink the traditional winter foods and beverages: *quentão*, a drink made of hot wines and ginger extract; *pinhão*, a pine nut which is first boiled and then cracked open, revealing a delicious white "meat" inside; and freshly popped popcorn.

Children enjoy the sights and sounds of firecrackers, sparklers, and fireworks during the June Festivals. People also release hundreds of miniature hot-air balloons. They are made of light wax paper and have a small hole at the bottom where a tiny candle is fastened. When the candle is lit, the balloon fills with hot air and rises into the cool night. In June the night sky is often dotted with the glowing balls of these balloons and the bright flashes of exploding fireworks.

Holidays to Remember

September 7 is Brazil's Independence Day. Brazilians celebrate the day in 1822 when Brazil won its independence from Portugal. The main colors of Brazil's flag—green and yellow—are everywhere. Gas station attendants attach green and yellow strips of plastic ribbon to cars' radio antennas. People wear green and yellow T-shirts. In most cities there are parades during the day. Schoolchildren march down the street following the school bands, fire and police departments display their equipment, and in major cities the armed forces will show their latest in tanks, rocket launchers, missiles, and other weaponry. It is a time for everyone to be proud of Brazil.

On November 2 Brazilians observe a serious occasion, the Day of the Dead. This is a quiet, sad day when people take flowers and candles to the cemetery to remember their loved ones who have died.

Brazilian Christmas traditions are similar to those of North Americans and Europeans. Christians attend special church services to celebrate the birth of Jesus. Stores are decorated with lights and tinsel, Christmas songs are played, and presents are exchanged. In the cities children flock to the shopping centers and department stores to see Santa Claus. During this holiday season, manger scenes of many shapes and sizes are displayed. One clay manger scene features Amazon Indians as Joseph, Mary, and the Baby Jesus!

Gifts for The Sea Goddess

Just a few days after Christmas, many Brazilians celebrate a religious tradition with African roots.

On New Year's Eve, these women and thousands of other Brazilian spiritists go to the beaches to offer gifts to Iemanjá, *the goddess of the sea.*

Although most Brazilians are Catholic, there are also many spiritists. On New Year's Eve, thousands of spiritists gather on many beaches along Brazil's Atlantic coast to pay tribute to *Iemanjá*, the goddess of the sea.

This night is a time to be thankful for the past year and to ask Iemanjá for her blessing during the next twelve months. Thousands of people, all dressed in white, go to the beaches carrying flowers and candles. They also bring gifts that a proud, beautiful woman would like to receive—combs, brushes, mirrors, and fine wines. Everything is placed on white tablecloths at the edge of the water. During the hours before midnight the people light candles, play drums, and sing and dance.

At exactly midnight, everyone suddenly runs into the ocean carrying their flowers and gifts for the goddess and throws them into the waves. If the gifts are washed away to sea, the giver relaxes and goes back home, confident that the new year will be good. If the waves toss a gift back toward the shore, it is considered a sign of bad luck.

Brazil's holidays reflect a mixture of many cultures and customs. People celebrate a traditional Christian holiday one week, and then offer gifts to a spiritist sea goddess the next. From Carnaval time in Rio to New Year's Eve on the beach, Brazilians celebrate their holidays with great enthusiasm and joy.

6. *Tropical Flavors*

What is the typical food of Brazil? Brazil is so big that each region has its own native specialties, which are mixed with dishes from other parts of Brazil or even from other countries.

A dish such as *vatapá* from the northeastern state of Bahia probably seems as foreign as Greek baklava to someone living in Rio Grande do Sul. But no matter where one goes in Brazil, the hospitality is the same. A popular proverb says that "In a mother's heart, there is always room for one more." This is especially true at the dinner table in Brazilian homes. One more person—a guest or neighbor—is always welcome.

Guests in a Brazilian home are reminded that they are welcome to stay as long as they would like. When a guest says it is time to leave, the host will usually protest, "*Está cedo!*" ("It's early!") even if it is already late at night. One way that Brazilians make their guests feel welcome is to offer them special foods from their region.

Regional Dishes

In the state of Bahia, a number of dishes consist of slices of plants, fish, or shrimp mixed together in red or

In parts of northeastern Brazil and the Amazon region, fish such as piranha is served along with other regional foods.

white sauces. These foods were first made centuries ago by the African slaves who were brought to Brazil to work on plantations. Since food was scarce in those days, slaves had to find scraps to eat. Soon they learned to mix these bits of vegetables, fish, chicken, and shrimp together, adding coconut milk or palm oil as a sauce. Today, although food is normally abundant, Bahians choose to make the dishes they have eaten all their lives.

One of the most popular Bahian dishes is vatapá. It

consists of pieces of shrimp and fish mixed with palm oil and coconut milk, and is served over white rice with pieces of bread. *Carurú* is a spicy dish with lots of fresh shrimp, okra bulbs, onions, red peppers, and hot sauce.

In the northern city of Belém, near the mouth of the Amazon River, a favorite dish is *pato no tucupi.* It is made of pieces of duck in a rich sauce with a wild green herb that tingles all the way down. Another local favorite is *tacacá* soup, a thick yellowish mixture containing dried shrimp and garlic.

In the southernmost state of Rio Grande do Sul, churrasco—chunks of beef pierced with a metal skewer and roasted over hot coals—is a favorite food. Usually the beef is marinated, or soaked, in a mixture of vinegar, lemon juice, and garlic. Churrasco is served with rice, potato salad, *polenta* (fried corn mush), or sometimes a fried banana, and makes a tasty and filling meal. Gaúchos, the cowboys of Rio Grande do Sul, take great pride in their knowledge of how to cut, prepare, and roast their churrasco.

After a good churrasco, many gaúchos like to sip chimarron tea. The tea leaves are placed inside a hollowed-out gourd, and then boiling water is poured over them. The gaúcho slowly sips the chimarron through a metal straw with a fine strainer on the lower tip.

Restaurants for Meat Eaters

When people go out to eat in Brazil, they often choose one of the country's thousands of *churrascarias*, restaurants that specialize in churrasco. In these popular eating places, no menu is needed. There is only one order—the works!

Soon after a group of people is seated, a waiter brings platters and bowls or rice, salads, beans, and other side dishes. Then the fun begins. Another waiter arrives with two long skewers, one filled with roasted sausage and the other with pieces of turkey wrapped in bacon. Then a third waiter arrives carrying a skewered ribroast. Every two minutes or so a waiter appears with a different cut of meat. He goes around the table, slicing slabs of meat right off the skewer and onto the plates of the restaurant's customers. At some churrascarias, as many as twenty types of meat are served. Churrascarias are usually housed in large buildings where dozens, and sometimes hundreds, of tables can be placed side by side. They are noisy, fun places where everyone has more than enough to eat.

A National Stew, Fruit, and Coffee

One of the few Brazilian dishes that is as popular in the south as in the north is *feijoada*, a thick stew of

Brazilians enjoy many varieties of mangoes, ranging from the tangy plum-sized type to the large red mango known as the coraçao de boi *("bull's heart").*

black beans to which pieces of pork are added as the mixture boils. The pork may vary in size from chips of bacon to pig's ears. Feijoada is usually served with white rice and manioc flour. It is garnished with a bit of *couve* (kale), a dark green leaf that is boiled and diced.

Just about every kind of fruit grows in Brazil, and Brazilians enjoy them all. Besides apples, oranges, peaches, strawberries, and bananas, such tropical fruits as papayas, mangoes, avocados, persimmons, cashew

In cities and villages all over Brazil, fruits and vegetables are sold in street markets called feiras.

fruit, and grapelike *jaboticabas* are widely available. These and many other fruits, as well as vegetables, flowers, and meats, are sold at street markets called *feiras.*

A feira is an open food market, held on roped-off city streets, that changes its location each day. On Monday it is in one part of town, Tuesday in another, and so on. Every day at closing time, the merchants take down their booths and pack up their fruit, until the next day when they will go to another neighborhood.

Though Brazil is the world's largest producer of coffee, not all of the coffee produced in the country is exported to other lands. Much of it remains at home, for Brazilians like coffee, too, and they make theirs dark, sweet, and strong. It is so strong that it is always served in very small cups. Usually one-third to one-half the cup is filled with sugar before the coffee is poured in. Even children drink coffee, normally in the morning with breakfast, and right after a meal.

Brazilian Meals

In Brazil a typical breakfast consists of a cup of *café com leite* (a hot milk and coffee mixture) and a piece of fresh French bread. Sometimes fruit or slices of ham and cheese are served as well. Most Brazilians consider breakfast to be just a snack meant to satisfy a person's hunger until lunchtime.

Almoço, or lunch, is usually the biggest meal of the day. For this meal, Brazilians will have rice, beans, salad, meat, or other dishes, depending on where they live and what they can afford to buy. In the evening a light supper is served in many homes.

In addition to lunch and dinner, generally served at noon and 7:30 P.M., some Brazilians have mid-morning and mid-afternoon *café*. The café includes not only coffee, but hot milk and cookies or bread as well.

Many Brazilians have a mid-morning or mid-afternoon café, *which is a light meal of cookies or bread and hot milk and coffee.*

Instead of the traditional café, many working Brazilians will stop in at snack shops called *pastelarias* for a quick bite between lunch and supper. These snack shops sell a variety of *salgadinhos*—hot "salties." Among the most popular items are *pastel*, fried dough usually filled with meat or cheese; *coxinha*, mashed dough and chicken meat served in the shape of a chicken thigh; *kibe*, a tasty Lebanese snack made of a fried meat and grain mixture; and *pão de queijo*, hot buns filled with melted cheese.

In Brazil, families don't always have meals together. Often individual schedules are considered more important than family mealtimes. In such families only special meals, such as Sunday dinner or meals with invited guests, are normally eaten together.

Nutrition and Favorite Foods

Until recently, most Brazilian parents were not particularly concerned about nutrition. They were more worried about having food on the table than about having a variety of the right kinds of foods to eat. Because parents did not know what foods their children needed, millions of young people developed serious diseases and other health problems. The situation has begun to change, as the government seeks to inform people about the importance of nutrition.

Like young people everywhere, Brazilian children enjoy sweets and desserts. One very popular dessert, *pudim*, is a thick, firm custard made from sweetened condensed milk and covered with melted sugar. Children also like *paçocas*, small candy bars made from crushed peanuts, and *churros*, fried dough rolled in sugar and filled with caramel, chocolate, or sweetened condensed milk. In Brazil's interior, the people often make candied desserts from potatoes, squash, or orange peels.

Despite all the tasty Brazilian foods available, people eat foods from all over the world as well. In addition to making churrasco and feijoada, many Brazilian cooks prepare Russian stroganoff, Italian spaghetti and meatballs, and American-style mashed potatoes.

The city of São Paulo has some of the world's best Italian restaurants. It is said that one can eat better Italian food in São Paulo than in Rome, Italy. U.S.-style fast-food restaurants are also popular among São Paulo's 8 million residents. In this city alone there are seventeen McDonald's restaurants!

Brazil's blending of national and foreign foods reflects the variety of the people who settled the many areas of South America's largest nation. The following recipes are fun to make and will give you a sample of some tasty Brazilian foods. The ingredients you will need are listed first, followed by the cooking instructions.

Avocado Soup

2 ripe avocados, peeled and cut into chunks
1/2 teaspoon salt
Dash of pepper

1 cup half-and-half cream
1 10-1/2 oz. can chicken broth
1 small avocado, thinly sliced

In blender, combine avocado chunks, salt, pepper, and half of the cream. Blend until smooth. Add remaining cream and blend just to mix. In large saucepan, bring chicken broth to boil. Stir in avocado mixture and remove from heat. Serve soup hot or cold, with sliced avocado on top.

Shrimp with Corn

2 pounds shrimp
3 tablespoons lemon juice
1/2 teaspoon salt
Dash of pepper
3 tablespoons butter or margarine
1 small onion, chopped
2-1/2 cups canned corn
12 black olives, pitted and chopped
1 cup sour cream

Wash the shrimp and place in a bowl. Add lemon juice, salt, and pepper. In a frying pan, melt butter and fry onion until golden. Add the shrimp and fry until pink. Add corn and olives. Cook for 2 minutes. Add sour cream, mix well. Remove from heat. Serve with white rice.

Pudim

1 pound sugar
1/2 tablespoon butter or margarine
1/2 cup water
6 egg yolks, beaten
1 cup shredded coconut

Grease one 10-12 muffin tin and sprinkle with a bit of sugar. In a saucepan, combine sugar and water. Bring to a boil, stirring until mixture forms a thin syrup. Add butter and remove from heat. When syrup is cold, add the egg yolks and coconut and mix well. Pour mixture into sections of muffin tin. Place tin in a pan filled with 1 inch of hot water. Bake in 350° oven for 30 to 40 minutes. They are finished when a toothpick inserted in the center comes out clean. When they are cool, invert the tin and turn out onto a large platter. Serve in bowls.

7. *School Life*

Imagine what it would be like if you weren't able to read. You would have to depend on others to read mail from friends and relatives. You could not understand street signs, billboards, license plates, store names, the newspaper, comic books, or even the writing on a cereal box. Most of the time you would feel as though you were completely in the dark.

Until recent years, more than half of Brazil's people found themselves in this situation. Some people were too poor to go to school—they had to spend all their time working in order to earn enough money to survive. Others lived in areas where there were no schools.

Then the Brazilian government discovered that people who cannot read have no way of making a better life for themselves. The government decided to spend more money to help these illiterate citizens receive a good education.

Many new schools were built, in the cities as well as in the villages and towns of Brazil's interior. The government even set up a national organization to teach illiterate adults how to read and write. Today, almost 80 percent of the Brazilian people can read and write, and children are required by law to attend school from ages seven to fourteen.

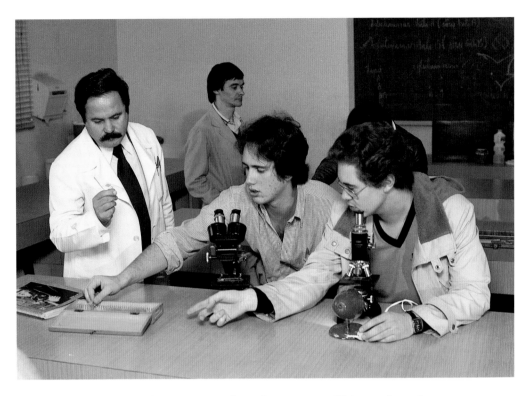

A high school science teacher shows two of his students how to conduct an experiment in the laboratory.

In Brazil's thousands of public schools, education is free. It is expensive for parents to send their children to private schools, but many do because the educational level at these schools is usually higher. Private schools often have more funds to spend on training teachers, buying equipment, building gymnasiums and laboratories, and developing good libraries.

Most Brazilian children begin school at age four, when many boys and girls are sent to *jardim da infância.* This is a type of kindergarten where they begin to learn to draw, to sing, and to play with other children. Here they become acquainted with colors, numbers, shapes, and the letters of the alphabet. At age five children go to *pré-primário*, or pre-grade school, for a year or two of learning more about the alphabet, numbers, basic reading, and arithmetic.

At age six or seven, regular grade school begins. The first eight years of schooling are called the *primeiro grau* ("first degree"). Afterwards students may go on to the *segundo grau* ("second degree"), or high school. Students who wish to attend college sign up for the *colegial* program, which prepares them for university studies. Students who are not interested in going to college may sign up for the *técnico* option. In this program they can begin to learn a profession, such as data processing, welding, or sewing.

In the first four years of primeiro grau, the students have one teacher for all subjects. Afterward, they usually have a different teacher for each subject. Whatever their grade, Brazilian children may choose whether they want to go to school during the morning or afternoon. From the fifth grade on, some students even have the option of attending classes at night. The morning session lasts from 7:00 to 11:30; the afternoon students go to school from 1:00 to 5:30. In this way, fewer schools can be used for more students.

A Day at School

What is a day at school like for a Brazilian boy or girl? To find out, let's look at the morning group of fourth-grade students at a public school in the city of Campinas. Before seven, the children begin to gather at the school gate. A high wall around the school grounds protects the school from thieves and other undesirable people.

All the children wear a school uniform, as they do every day. The boys dress in white shirts and navy-blue pants, while the girls have white blouses and blue pleated skirts. Both boys and girls wear black shoes.

Everyone carries a backpack or another type of bag that holds schoolbooks, notebooks, and school materials. Unlike schools in North America, where textbooks normally are the property of the school, students buy their books at the beginning of the semester.

Just before seven the gate opens. The boys and girls file past the guard at the gate, who makes sure that everyone is wearing a proper, clean uniform. Today the children line up outside the school building in front of a tall flagpole bearing the green, yellow, blue, and white Brazilian flag. Together they put their right hands over

Young people exercise during a physical education class. Many of Brazil's schools do not have the needed equipment and gymnasiums for physical education and sports.

their hearts and sing all the verses of the *"Hino Nacional,"* the national anthem of Brazil. Then they all go to their classrooms.

When they have settled into their seats, the fourth-grade *professora*, or teacher, opens her attendance book and reads the students' names. After each name, a child responds with, *"Presente."*

Today she asks them to take out their Portuguese notebooks and practice writing words that contain the nasal *ão* sound. She begins writing the words on the board, and the children repeat after her: "*Pão, mão, são, mamão, chão.* . ." The professora reminds them that the funny-looking squiggly accent must always be put over the letter *a* in such words.

Then she reads them a story from a book by Brazilian author José de Alencar. After she reads the story, she asks the class to prepare for a *ditado* ("dictation"). The professora selects a paragraph from the book, and begins to read it very slowly. The children copy every word into their notebooks as she speaks. When they are finished, they tear out the sheets from their notebooks, write their names at the top, and hand them in to the teacher for grading.

Next it is time for arithmetic class, and the students take their arithmetic notebooks out of their bags. The professora writes a few multiplication problems on the board and asks her students to solve them. After completing the problems and handing in their assignments, together they recite the multiplication tables.

At recess the children are allowed to play outside for twenty minutes. Some of them play *rela-rela*, or tag. Others buy popsicles or popcorn from street vendors the guard has allowed to enter the school grounds. When the bell rings, the children straighten their clothes and go inside to begin their lessons again.

The professora has a surprise for her students. She tells them that a field trip is being arranged to the zoo the following week. When they return, she says, they will have to write a short composition about their favorite animal.

Social studies is the last subject of the day. The professora tells the class that today they will begin to study about a faraway country in North America—the United States. She tells them that the United States is one of the world's largest and most important countries. The students open their books and begin to read the first few paragraphs of the chapter. The professora asks each child to read a few sentences and then hands out maps of the United States. The homework assignment, she explains, is to write in the names of ten American cities on this map next to the corresponding dots already drawn in.

When the 11:30 bell rings, the children stuff their books and notebooks into their knapsacks and backpacks and run out the door. Their school day has ended.

A Difficult Test

After Brazilian students have completed both the first and second degree programs, they may wish to attend one of Brazil's sixty-five colleges and universities.

In order to get into college, students must first pass a difficult test called the *vestibular*. This examination tests students' knowledge of biology, chemistry, physics, math, Portuguese, English, and several other subjects. Young men and women who do not pass this exam must study hard and take it again in six months. Some students pass the vestibular the first time they try. Others may take as long as four or five years before they pass it.

To help students study for the vestibular, many private schools called *cursinhos* have been founded. Students in such schools have to study hard and long and often work until late at night. When the time comes to take the test, they try to remember everything they have studied for the past six months.

The results of the vestibular are usually made known within a day or two. Those who pass this all-important test are immediately "initiated" by upperclass students. To initiate a young man, other students rip up his clothes, throw paint and mud on him, and cut off chunks of his hair. A young woman is painted and covered with mud. Then all the students who passed the test are marched downtown to celebrate. After it is all over, the young men usually go to a barbershop to have the rest of their hair shaved off. In the days following the tests, others know that the bald students are the successful ones.

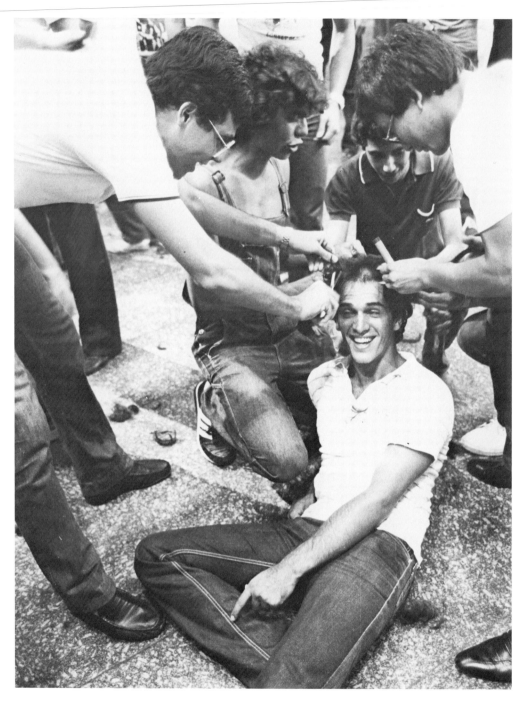

When a student passes the college entrance examination, he or she is "initiated" by upperclass students. This young man has had his hair cut off.

Problems and Promise

Because Brazil is not a rich country, it does not have a great deal of money to spend on improving education. Many of the school buildings are old and in need of repair. Most schools do not have libraries, laboratories, or gyms for physical education classes. The government has had a hard time finding qualified teachers to work in the schools, because salaries for teachers are very low.

Although Brazil now has enough schools for its children, millions of very poor boys and girls still don't go to school because they must earn money during the day to buy enough food for a meal. The government is trying to change this situation, but it has a long way to go. Crowded city slums, unemployed workers, and abandoned children all contribute to the problems faced by millions of young people.

Even though Brazil's schools and students have many problems, the government is doing as much as it can to offer an effective educational program to its people. It has recently begun to provide free lunches for poor students. In addition, it has increased the funds made available to universities for use in research. Brazil's government has learned that the best way to prepare for the future is to educate its people well.

8. Soccer Fever

Here are some facts that will help you identify Brazil's most popular sport.

- According to most experts, the best soccer player who ever lived is Pelé, a Brazilian.
- Brazil has more professional soccer teams than any other country in the world.
- The world's largest soccer stadium is the Maracanã, located in Rio de Janeiro; it seats 200,000 fans.

Soccer Country

All these facts, and many more like them, show that Brazil is soccer country. Unlike other countries, where a different sport is featured each season, in Brazil soccer is played all year long. Counting the state, regional, and national championships, hundreds of matches are played each year. That total does not take into account the many international cups and tournaments that Brazil participates in regularly, including the world's largest single-sport tournament—the World Cup.

When a boy is born in Brazil, often the first gift he receives is a soccer ball. If he is like most other boys, in his first few years of life he learns how to kick, dribble,

Thousands of soccer fans watch the exciting action during a match between Corinthians and Vasco da Gama, two professional teams.

and handle the ball with his feet. While he is still very young, he learns the simple rules of the game. By the age of eight, he can handle the ball well and plays on school soccer fields, vacant lots, and even on the streets.

Older boys who show promise as soccer players are often sent to train with junior league teams, which serve as training centers for professional clubs. There the young players learn the finer points of the game, and a few go on to play professional ball.

Brazil has produced some of the world's best soccer players. Names such as Carlos Alberto, Garrincha, Tostão, Jairzinho, and Zico are legendary in international soccer. Pelé—whose real name is Edson Arantes do Nascimento—stands out among all of Brazil's great stars. His perfect style and extraordinary skills were matched only by his ability to sense where the ball—and his fellow teammates—would be in the next second.

In Brazil every soccer fan has a favorite team. The people of São Paulo might root for the home teams of Palmeiras, Corínthians, or Portuguesa. Cariocas choose among Fluminense, Flamengo, Botafogo, Bangú, and the other professional teams of Rio. Almost every one of Brazil's states has at least one professional team.

Brazilian soccer fans know how to cheer on their team, and they do it in some unusual and noisy ways. Fans wave large flags in the stadiums, shoot off hundreds of firecrackers, yell, hiss, and whistle at every success or error on the field. The crowd jumps for joy whenever a goal is scored, and samba music plays nonstop in the stands. It is not unusual for a fan to go home more tired than the soccer player himself!

For Brazilian soccer fans, one competition stands out among all others—the World Cup. Because it is held every four years, this worldwide championship is considered the Olympics of soccer. Brazil traditionally

Many fans and players regard Pelé as the greatest soccer player in the history of the game. During his career, he scored more than a thousand goals and led Brazil to three World Cup championships.

Soccer fans wave flags during a match in the huge Maracanã stadium in Rio de Janeiro.

ranks among the best teams of the world. So far there have been thirteen World Cups, and Brazil has won three of them.

During the month-long World Cup games, there is a feeling of excitement all over Brazil. The colors of Brazil—yellow, green, and blue—are displayed everywhere. When Brazil plays a World Cup match, the whole country shuts down to watch the game. Banks, public office buildings, and stores actually close their doors during the match so that their employees can watch it. If Brazil wins, the entire nation celebrates. People run out of their homes waving enormous flags, and on the road they flash their lights and honk their horns. Boys run outside and try to imitate their favorite players in a neighborhood soccer game. They pretend they are playing for their national team in a World Cup game.

Race Cars and Beach Games

In addition to soccer, many Brazilians are fans of auto racing. In recent years several Brazilian race-car drivers have participated in the Grand Prix racing circuit. Emerson Fittipaldi was the world champion in 1972 and 1974. Another Brazilian, Nelson Piquet, won the Grand Prix championship in 1981.

Millions of Brazilians follow the annual worldwide circuit of Grand Prix races. All of the races are broadcast live on Brazilian television. The yearly Brazilian Grand Prix race is held at either the Interlagos Raceway in São Paulo or the Jacarepaguá Raceway in Rio de Janeiro.

A sport that has become more popular in recent years is volleyball. Traditionally considered a women's sport, more and more men have begun to play the game as well. Brazil possesses one of the world's best men's national volleyball teams, and women's volleyball is not

During the Brazilian Grand Prix, race cars speed down the track at Rio de Janeiro's Jacarepaguá Raceway.

far behind. Their quick, intelligent style of playing makes them extremely difficult to beat. Many young people play the game just for fun at the beach.

Going to the beach is a favorite activity for millions of Brazilians who live near the ocean. Brazil has thousands of miles of Atlantic coastline and hundreds of beautiful beaches. During the summer months of December, January, and February, many of these beaches are crowded with vacationers.

For many Brazilians, the beach is a place to wind-surf, hang-glide, play beach soccer or volleyball, or just lie in the sun.

For the residents of Rio de Janeiro and other coastal cities, the beach has become a way of life. All day long young people surf and sail-surf on the waves and soar above the sand and sea in colorful hang-gliders.

Private Clubs and Public Parks

Brazil does not have a large number of public swimming pools, soccer fields, and tennis courts. As a result, middle- and upper-class Brazilian families often join clubs that have all of these things and much more. During the evening hours and weekends, these clubs are usually packed with fun-seekers. They are especially popular in the cities of Brazil's interior, where there are no natural beaches or recreation areas.

Not all sports and recreational activities happen on beaches or in private clubs. Most cities in Brazil have at least one public park where people can go to walk, run, bicycle, or simply enjoy the natural surroundings. Parts of these large parks contain acres of the area's natural vegetation. In fact, it is not uncommon to see several blocks of "jungle" in the middle of a downtown area. Such parks are sometimes called "the poor man's club," because people don't have to pay an entrance fee to use them. And yet, parks such as Rio's beautiful Jardim Botânico or São Paulo's Parque Ibirapuera attract the rich and poor alike.

Any Brazilian can take part in the annual marathon and mini-marathon races run in the larger cities. The most well known is São Paulo's São Silvestre race, which is run on New Year's Eve. Each year many thousands of runners come from all parts of Brazil to run in the São Silvestre. Even world champion runners participate, and the race is open to anyone, regardless of nationality. Those who finish the exciting mini-marathon course experience the thrill of running into the

New Year along São Paulo's most fashionable avenue, Avenida Paulista.

A Native Brazilian Sport

One fascinating sport, *capoeira*, is native to Brazil. This striking blend of fighting and dancing originated in Brazil's northeastern states, among the slaves that had been brought from Africa. According to historians, slaves were ordered by their "masters" not to fight one another. If they were caught fighting, they were severely punished.

Despite the threat of punishment, a slave who was insulted or offended by a fellow slave wanted to avenge himself. He would challenge the person who had wronged him to a duel. Such a duel was carefully disguised by other slaves who knew about the dispute. First, a group of slaves gathered in a large circle. Some of the people in the circle had the job of looking out for the master. A musician in the group played the *berimbau*, an instrument made of a bow fastened to a hollow gourd and tied with a piece of metal wire. The musician tapped the wire with a copper coin to produce a peculiar twanging sound, while in his other hand he shook a small, seed-filled rattle. In perfect time with the music, the dueling slaves began to fight, using hands, elbows, feet, and knees to land blows on each other.

If the master approached, the fighters were quietly warned. Without so much as missing a step, they continued their flailing movements, but this time without hitting each other. They leaped high into the air and descended just inches away from their "partner's" jaw or stomach. The master, then, thought the slaves were just practicing a strange African dance, never realizing that the moment he looked away the kicks and punches would suddenly become very real.

Over the years this fight-dance was perfected and became a Brazilian art form. Today capoeira is no longer used as a fighting disguise. It is a sport requiring great physical skill as well as agility and control. Brazilians spend hours at a time listening to the berimbau and watching the powerful yet delicate dance of capoeira.

From private clubs to public parks and beaches, Brazilians have many places to participate in sports and recreational activities. And from the Maracanã stadium to the back streets and vacant lots of crowded cities and remote villages, soccer fever runs high.

9. New Life in a New Home

For more than four hundred years, Brazil has attracted emigrants from all over the world. First came the Portuguese, and then other Europeans, Africans, Asians, Middle Easterners, and other Latin Americans. Brazil has been and continues to be a country *to which* people move. Although thousands of Brazilians work, study, or vacation in many countries of the world, very few have given up their citizenship.

Only about 55,000 Brazilian immigrants now live in the United States. This is just a tiny fraction of the number of people who have come from other lands. A number of countries that are much smaller than Brazil have many more U.S. immigrants.

Why Brazilians Stay Home

Why are there so few Brazilian immigrants in the United States? There are several reasons. First, Brazilians seem more willing to endure difficult conditions than the people of many other countries. When people in other lands experienced hardships, they often chose to go to America, the land of hope and opportunity. People did exactly that, and they came by the millions.

The faces of these young women show the origins of some of the emigrants who have come to Brazil from all over the world.

In Brazil, though, when the going gets tough, as it often does, the people usually look around for ways to solve their problems at home. The thought of leaving Brazil and family and friends does not occur naturally. The Brazilians have an old saying: *Deus é brasileiro* ("God is a Brazilian"), and strongly believe it. They think that with a little more hope, patience, or time, things will get better.

Another reason Brazilians have not left for the

United States is that they have not been able to pay the price of boat or plane tickets for themselves and their families. Even today, most Brazilians cannot afford to emigrate.

A third reason has to do with Brazil's enormous size. The country itself is so big that people never feel they have quite run out of possibilities. For example, if a family living in the northeastern state of Sergipe experiences great hardships, the parents may decide to move to the city of Salvador in the state of Bahia. If things don't work out there, they can always move to São Paulo, thousands of miles to the south. And if things don't work out there, perhaps they could try one of the newly developed regions of Brazil's interior.

From the family's point of view, it is much easier to move to a city in the same country than to an entirely new country. That way the family does not have to adjust to a new language, a new culture, and a new way of life. Brazil is so enormous that most Brazilians see it as being several "countries" within one.

Even though there are few immigrants from Brazil in North America, the people of Brazil respect and admire the United States. They are impressed by American science and technology, and are influenced by American culture. Just as in the United States, Brazilian young people wear blue jeans, eat hamburgers, drink Coca-Cola, and listen to rock'n'roll. Most Brazilians are

Far from the cities along Brazil's coast, people have cleared land for farms and ranches in the nation's vast interior regions.

interested in learning to speak English, because it is an international language widely used in business and education. Small children are sometimes sent to schools where they can start learning English at an early age.

Brazilian Culture in the United States

Just as U.S. culture influences life in Brazil, examples of Brazilian culture are present in the United States.

Movies, such as *Dona Flor and Her Two Husbands* and *Kiss of the Spider Woman* have been successful in the United States. The most famous Brazilian actress, Sonia Braga, was born to a poor family living in the interior town of Maringá. Her family moved to Rio de Janeiro while she was still young. Through hard work and talent, Braga became a great star. Before becoming a movie actress, she was the hostess of the Brazilian version of the "Sesame Street" TV program!

The music of Brazil is heard widely throughout the United States and Canada. In the early 1960s, Brazilian musicians introduced *bossa nova* to American and Canadian audiences, and this new style of music became instantly successful. Bossa nova music needs few instruments—an acoustic guitar, a bass guitar, drums, piano, and a flute—but its catchy rhythms are infectious. Similar to bossa nova are samba and *samba canção*, a mellow version of the Carnaval music. Musicians and bands such as Antonio Carlos Jobim, Egberto Gismonti, Sérgio Mendes and Brazil '88, João Gilberto, Airto Moreira, Naná Vasconcelos, and Milton Nascimento are among the best-known Brazilians in international jazz circles.

More and more North Americans are beginning to read books written by Latin American authors. One of the best-selling authors is Jorge Amado, who has written many novels about life in the north of Brazil.

Among his most well known books are *Gabriela: Clove and Cinnamon* and *Captains of Sand*. Other Brazilian authors that have had books translated into English are Ignácio de Loyola Brandão, Paulo Freire, Gilberto Freyre, and Dom Helder Câmara.

Never have there been more Brazilian products for sale in North America than there are now. Most of the fine-quality Brazilian shoes shipped to the United States and Canada are made in the southern city of Franca, where there are dozens of shoe factories, large and small. Every year North Americans buy large amounts of coffee, soybean products, and orange juice from Brazil. They also purchase such exports as automobiles, trucks, and military aircraft.

Looking to the Future

As Brazilians themselves admit, their country is far from perfect. Most of their people are very poor, and can barely afford to meet their basic needs for food and shelter from one month to the next. Their cities suffer from pollution and crime, and their government officials have not always served the best interests of the people.

And yet, even the poorest Brazilians often look a little further down the road than today or tomorrow. They look into the future, to the day when Brazil, with

Standing with outstretched arms atop Rio de Janeiro's Corcovado Mountain, the Christ the Redeemer statue is a symbol of hope, comfort, and opportunity for immigrants arriving in Brazil.

all its rich natural and human resources, finally becomes what it can be.

When immigrants come into the United States at New York Harbor, they see the welcoming sight of the Statue of Liberty. Standing tall in the harbor, it promises life, liberty, and justice to all. When immigrants arrive by boat or plane in Rio de Janeiro, they are likely to see the outstretched arms of the Christ the Redeemer statue, standing atop the nearby mountain. It, too, is a symbol of hope, comfort, and opportunity for those who have come seeking a new life in a new home.

Appendix

Brazilian Consulates in the United States and Canada

The Brazilian consulates in the United States and Canada offer assistance and information about all aspects of Brazilian life. For information and resource materials about Brazil, contact the embassy or consulate nearest you.

U.S. Consulates and Embassy

Atlanta, Georgia
Brazilian Consulate and
    Trade Bureau
229 Peachtree Street, Northeast
Suite 2420
Atlanta, Georgia 30303
Phone (221) 659-0660

Chicago, Illinois
Brazilian Consulate and
    Trade Bureau
20 North Wacker Drive
Suite 530
Chicago, Illinois 60606
Phone (312) 372-2190

Dallas, Texas
Brazilian Consulate
World Trade Center
2050 Stemmons Freeway
Suite 174
Dallas, Texas 75258
Phone (214) 651-1854

Houston, Texas
Brazilian Consulate
1333 West Loop South
Suite 1100
Houston, Texas 77027
Phone (713) 961-3063

Los Angeles, California
Brazilian Consulate General
5900 Wilshire Boulevard
Suite 650
Los Angeles, California 90036
Phone (213) 937-4044

Miami, Florida
Brazilian Consulate and
    Trade Bureau
100 North Biscayne Boulevard
Suite 2113
Miami, Florida 33132
Phone (305) 377-1734

New Orleans, Louisiana
Brazilian Consulate General
2 Canal Street
International Trade Mart
  Building
Suite 1306
New Orleans, Louisiana 70130
Phone (504) 588-9187

New York, New York
Brazilian Consulate General
630 Fifth Avenue
27th Floor
New York, New York 10111
Phone (212) 757-3080

San Francisco, California
Brazilian Consulate
300 Montgomery Street
Suite 1160
San Francisco, California 94104
Phone (415) 981-8170

Washington, D.C.
Brazilian Embassy and
  Trade Bureau
3006 Massachusetts Avenue,
  Northwest
Washington, D.C. 20008
Phone (202) 797-0100

Canadian Consulates and Embassy

Montreal, Quebec
Consulat General du Bresil
  et Bureau Commercial
1, Place Ville Marie
Suite 1505
Montreal, Quebec H3B 2B5
Phone (514) 866-3313

Ottawa, Ontario
Brazilian Embassy and
  Trade Bureau
255 Albert Street
Suite 900
Ottawa, Ontario K1P 6A9
Phone (613) 237-1090

Toronto, Ontario
Brazilian Consulate and
  Trade Bureau
130 Floor Street West
Room 617
Toronto, Ontario M5S 1N5
Phone (416) 921-4534

Glossary

almoço (ahl·MOH·soh)—mid-day dinner; lunch

baião (by·OWN)—music from Brazil's Northeast, featuring tambourines and accordions

bandeirantes (buhn·day·RUHN·teez)—the flag bearers who marked off the boundaries of Brazil

berimbau (bair·ihm·BOW)—a bowlike stringed musical instrument used to accompany the *capoeira* dance

Bicho Papão (BEE·shoh pah·POWN)—the Brazilian "boogey man"

bossa nova (BAW·suh NAW·vuh)—music resembling the samba with jazz influences

Buraco Quente (boo·RAH·koo KEHN·tee)—a particularly crime-ridden favela in São Paulo

café (kah·FAY)—coffee; also refers to the mid-morning or mid-afternoon snack time

café com leite (kah·FAY cohn LAY·tee)—a hot milk and coffee beverage

candomblé (kuhn·dohm·BLAY)—a spiritist religion that combines African spiritual beliefs with Catholicism

capoeira (kah·poh·AY·ruh)—a traditional fight/dance, originally practiced by African slaves, that has become a Brazilian art form

carioca (kah·ree·AW·kuh)—a resident of Rio de Janeiro

Carnaval (kahr·nah·VAHL)—Mardi Gras; the joyous, nonstop celebration just before Ash Wednesday

carurú (kah·roo·ROO)—a heavily spiced dish made with shrimp, okra, and peppers

chimarron (shee·mah·HOHN)—a strong tea made of *mate* leaves

churrascaria (shoo·hahs·kah·REE·uh)—a restaurant that specializes in skewered meats

churrasco (shoo·HAHS·koh)—barbecued meat seasoned with salt and spices

churros (SHOO·hoos)—fried dough rolled in crystallized sugar and filled with caramel or sweetened condensed milk

Cidade Maravilhosa (see·DAH·dee mah·rah·veel·YAW·zuh)—"Marvelous City"; Rio de Janeiro

colegial (cohl·ehzh·ee·AHL)—a college preparatory high school option

couve (KOH·vee)—kale; a dark green, leafy vegetable often served with *feijoada*

coxinha (koh.SHEEN·yuh)—mashed dough and chicken meat, served in the shape of a chicken thigh

cuíca (koo·EE·kuh)—a drum-shaped musical instrument used to produce a yelping, whelping sound

cursinho (koor·SEEN·yoh)—a private school which prepares students for the college entrance examination

ditado (dee·TAH·doh)—a dictation

favela (fah·VEH·luh)—a slum of Brazil's big cities

feijoada (fayzhoh·AH·duh)—a thick, black-bean stew containing pieces of pork

feira (FAY·ruh)—an open street market where fruit and vegetables are sold

futebol (foo·teh·BAWL)—soccer

garimpeiros (gah·reen·PAY·rohz)—independent prospectors who pan for gold in the Amazon region

gaúcho (gah·OO·shoh)—a "cowboy" from southern Brazil

guaraná (gwah·rah·NAH)—a soft drink made from the juice of a red berry that grows in Amazonas

Iemanjá (yay·muhn·ZHAH)—for spiritists, the goddess of the seas

Instituto Butantan (een·stee·TOO·too boo·tuhn·TUHN) —a São Paulo snake farm and research center where poisonous snakes are "milked" for their venom

jaboticaba (zhah·boh·tee·KAH·buh)—a grapelike, strong-tasting fruit

jardim da infância (zhar·DEEN dah een·FUHN·see·uh) kindergarten

kibe (KEE·bee)—a Lebanese food popular in Brazil; it consists of a deep-fried meat and wheat mixture

Lei Áurea (lay OW·ree·uh)—a law signed in 1888 granting freedom to Brazil's slaves

macumba (mah·KOOM·bah)—a spiritist religion that

combines African spiritual beliefs with Catholicism

nordeste (nawr·DEHS·tee)—the dry, arid Northeast region of Brazil

nordestino (nawr·dehs·TEE·noh)—a resident of the *nordeste*

Nova República (naw·vuh reh·POO·blee·kuh)—the "New Republic"; term used to refer to Brazil's new democratic political system

novela (noh·VEH·luh)—television soap operas, which are very popular in Brazil

onça (OHN·suh)—a spotted leopard

paçoca (pah·SAW·kuh)—a peanut candy bar

pagode (pah·GAW·dee)—a samba-based style of music featuring multiple vocals

pão de queijo (pown·dee KAYzhoh)—cheese bread

pastel (pahs·TEHL)—deep-fried dough filled with meat, cheese, or heart-of-palm

pastelaria (pahs·tehl·ah·REE·uh)—an eating place specializing in deep-fried salty snacks

pato no tucupi (PAH·toh noh too·koo·PEE)—a dish made from duck meat and green herbs

pau brasil (pow brah·ZEEL)—brazilwood; an early name for the land that became the nation of Brazil

pinhão (peen·YOWN)—a pine nut containing a tasty white "meat"

piranha (pee·RUHN·yuh)—small but deadly meat-eating fish found in the rivers of northern Brazil

pirarucú (pee·rah·roo·KOO)—a very large fish found in the Amazon River

polenta (poh·LEHN·tuh)—fried corn mush

pré-primário (preh·pree·MAH·ree·oh)—preschool

primeiro grau (pree·MAY·roh GROW)—the first eight years of public school

professora (proh·feh·SOH·ruh)—a female teacher

pudim (poo·DEEN)—a thick custard made from sweet-ened condensed milk and covered with melted sugar

quadrilha (kwah·DREEL·yuh)—a square dance

quentão (kehn·TOWN)—an alcoholic beverage made of hot wine and ginger extract

Reforma Agrária (reh·FAWR·muh uh·GRAH·ree·uh)—a government program that takes unused land from wealthy landowners and gives it to poor farmers who agree to farm it

rela-rela (heh·luh·HEH·luh)—a game of tag

Saci-Pererê (sah·SEE·peh·reh·REH)—the mischievous one-legged, pipe-smoking creature of Brazilian myths and legends

salgadinhos (sahl·gah·DEEN·yohz)—salty snacks made of fried dough and meat combinations

samba (SUHM·buh)—the rhythmic music of Carnaval

samba-canção (suhm·buh kuhn·SOWN)—a mellow ver-sion of samba, featuring slow rhythms and guitar

segundo grau (seh·GOON·doh GROW)—the last three

years of public school

seringueiro (seh·reen·GAY·roh)—a person who extracts sap from rubber trees in Brazil's Amazon region

sertaneja (sehr·tah·NAY·zhuh)—mournful music in which balladeers sing about lost loves

tacacá (tah·kah·KAH)—a thick yellow soup containing dried shrimp and garlic

técnico (TEHK·nee·koh)—a job training program for high school students who choose not to go to college

Tiradentes (tee·rah·DEHN·tees)—the "Tooth Puller"; the nickname of Joaquim José da Silva Xavier, an eighteenth century Brazilian freedom fighter and martyr

trombadinha (trohm·bah·DEEN·yuh)—"little crash"; used to refer to young thieves and pickpockets

vatapá (vah·tah·PAH)—a shrimp-based spicy stew from the state of Bahia

vestibular (vehs·tee·boo·LAHR)—the Brazilian college entrance examination

vitória régia (vee·TAW·ree·uh REH·zhee·uh)—giant lily pads of northern Brazil's rivers

Selected Bibliography

Bennett, Olivia. *A Family in Brazil.* Minneapolis: Lerner, 1986.

Cleveland, James Allen. *Brazilian Odyssey.* Ardmore, Pennsylvania: Dorrance & Company, 1981.

Laver, Ross. Beginning Anew in Brazil. *MacLeans* (January 21, 1985): 24-26.

Main, J. Brazil's Tomorrow Is Finally in Sight. *Fortune* (September 15, 1986): 72-78.

Roett, R. The Transition to Democracy in Brazil. *Current History* (January 1986): 21-24.

Sarney, J. Brazil: A President's Story. *Foreign Affairs* (Fall 1986): 101-117.

Vesilind, Priit J. Brazil: Moment of Promise and Pain. *National Geographic* (March 1987): 348-385.

Williams, J.H. Men of Iron, Dreams of Gold. *Americas* (May-June 1985): 20-23.

Index

About the Author

Currently executive director of Editora Mundo Cristão, a religious publishing house in São Paulo, Mark Carpenter is completely at home in Brazil. He lived in Brazil from the time he was three until he was twenty-one, and returned to the United States to attend college and work as a writer and editor. Since he grew up in Brazil and now works there, Mr. Carpenter considers himself to be totally bicultural.

This book, says the author, "will help North American young people to understand Brazil from the standpoint of a Brazilian. It will encourage them to respect and admire the resilience, dignity, and warmth of the Brazilian people."

Mr. Carpenter is also the author of *Carlos*, a book about the abandoned street children of São Paulo, and serves as the Brazilian correspondent for *Christianity Today*. He and his wife and child reside in São Paulo.